Five Orchestral Pieces
and
Pelleas und Melisande

IN FULL SCORE

ARNOLD SCHOENBERG

DOVER PUBLICATIONS, INC.
NEW YORK

Bibliographical Note

This Dover edition, first published in 1994, is a republication in one volume of two works originally published in separate editions. *Pelleas und Melisande: Symphonische Dichtung für Orchester op. 5 Nach dem Drama von Maurice Maeterlinck* was originally published by Universal Edition, A. G., Vienna, 1912. *Fünf Orchesterstücke von Arnold Schönberg, Opus 16*, was originally published by C. F. Peters, Leipzig, 1912. The Dover edition adds an overall contents page, an instrumentation list for each work and a glossary of German terms in both scores, including translations of footnotes and longer score notes.

Library of Congress Cataloging-in-Publication Data

Schoenberg, Arnold, 1874–1951.
    [Stücke, orchestra, op. 16]
    Five orchestral pieces ; and, Pelleas und Melisande, op. 5 / Arnold Schoenberg.—In full score.
    1 score.
    Pelleas und Melisande is a symphonic poem.
    Originally published: Leipzig : C. F. Peters, 1912 (Pieces); Vienna: Universal Edition, 1912 (Pelleas).
    ISBN 0-486-28120-5
    1. Orchestral music—Scores. 2. Symphonic poems—Scores. I. Schoenberg, Arnold, 1874–1951. Pelleas und Melisande. 1994. II. Title: Pelleas und Melisande.
    M1000.S36   1994   94-8466
                                                          CIP
                                                         M

Manufactured in the United States of America
Dover Publications, Inc., 31 East 2nd Street, Mineola, N.Y. 11501

Contents

Glossary of German Terms
Translations of footnotes and longer score notes appear at the end of this section.

aber, but, though
alle, all *(tutti)*
alle mit Bog(en), all play with the bow *(tutti arco)*
alle 3 [4, etc.] mit Dpf. [Dämpfer], all 3 [etc.] muted
allein, alone (solo)
als, to
als Auftakt zu spielen, to be played as an upbeat
am Steg, on the bridge *(sul ponticello)*
A Seite, on the A string *(sul A)*
auf beiden Fellen, on both heads [of the timpani]
auf beiden Pkn. [Pauken], on both timpani
auf der C [D, etc.] Saite, on the C [etc.] string *(sul C)*
auf 2 Saiten, on two strings
ausdrucksvoll, expressively

B [also, *in B*], B-flat
Bassstimme, bass voice [lowest part]
*Beck(en) mit dem [also, m. d.] Schlägel [also, Paukenschläge*l],
   cymbals (played) with beaters [timpani sticks]
beschleunigend, accelerating *(accelerando)*
bewegt(er), (more) moving, agitated
bewegte Achtel, moving 8th notes
Bog(en), bow, bowed *(arco)*
breit(er), broad(er)
[aber] breit im Ton, [but] with a broad sound

Cis, C-sharp
C Saite, on the C string *(sul C)*

D(ämpfer), mute
Dämpfer ab, mute off
Dämpfer auf(setzen), mute on
Dämpfer [also, Dpf.] weg, remove the mute
das tiefe es, the low E-flat
der, of the
deutlich (hervortr.), distinct, clear (to the fore)
die, the
die andere Hälfte, the other half [of the section]
die eine Hälfte, (the one) half [of the section]
die Hälfte, half [of the section]
die übrigen get(eilt), the others divided *(gli altri, divisi)*
Doppelgriff, doublestop
D Saite, on the D string *(sul D)*
dünn, flimsy, thin

Echotonartig, like an echo
ein, one
ein wenig bewegt(er), slightly animated
ein wenig hervortretend, slightly to the fore
4 einzelne Vcll., 4 (individual) cellos
Es, E-flat
E Saite, on the E string *(sul E)*
etwas, somewhat, slightly
etwas belebter, slightly more lively
etwas bewegt(er), somewhat (more) animated
etwas langsamer, a little slower
etwas rascher, somewhat quicker
etwas zurückhaltend, slightly held back
eventuell Flag(eolett), possible harmonics

4 [3, etc.] fach get(eilt), divided into 4 [etc.] parts *(divisi a4)*
Fis, F-sharp
Flag(eolett), harmonic
Flag(eolett) auf der E [etc.] Saite, harmonic on the E [etc.] string
Flatterzunge, fluttertongue
fünfsaitig Solo-Kb. [Solo-Kontrabasse], five-string solo bass

gebunden, legato
gedämpft, muted (for horn), damped (for timpani)
gest(opft), stopped (for horn)
get(eilt), divided *(divisi)*
Gis, G-sharp
gleiche Teile, equal parts
Griffbrett, fingerboard
G Saite, on the G string *(sul G)*

H, B-natural
Hälfte, half [of the section]
Haltung, hold *(fermata)*
hart, rough, harsh
hastig, hurried
heftig(er), (more) violent, fervent
hell, distinct, brilliant
hervor(tretend), prominent, to the fore

immer, always, steadily
immer steigernd, steadily louder *(sempre crescendo)*
im Zeitmass, in tempo
in gehender Bewegung, at a walking pace
in 4 [etc.] Teilen, in 4 [etc.] parts

Klang, tone [actual sound of harmonic]
kurz(e), short

lang, long, prolonged
langsam(er), slow(er)
langsamer werdend (und abnehmend), becoming slower
   (and quieter)
lebhaft, lively
leicht (ein wenig hervortr[etend]), lightly (a bit to the fore)

mässige Viertel, moderate quarter notes
m(it), with
mit Dämpfer, muted *(con sordino)*
   [also appears as: *mit Dämpf., m. Dpf.,*
   m. d(er) Dpf., mit D. and *m. D.*]
m(it) d(em) Schlägel, with beaters
mit grossem Ausdruck, with great expression
Mittelstimme, middle voice [of the ensemble]

nach u(nd) nach, little by little, gradually
   [See "Other Tempo Markings" at the end of the glossary]
Nebenstimme, secondary (accompanying) voice
nicht, not
nicht gebunden, not legato
nicht get(eilt), undivided *(non divisi)*
nimmt, change to [a different instrument]
nur 3 [4, etc.], only 4 [etc.] players

offen, open (for brass)
o(hne), without
ohne Dämpfer, without mute *(senza sordino)*
    [also appears as: *ohne Dpf., o. Dpf.* and *o. D.*]
ohne Nachschlag trillern, trill without Nachschlag

Paukenschlägel, timpani sticks
Pult(e), desk(s) [of the orchestra]

rasch, quick
rasch anschwellend, getting louder quickly
ruhig, calm

Schalltr(ichter) hoch, put the bell [of the instrument] in the air
scharf, biting, piercing
schreiend, screaming
sehr, very
sehr ausdrucksvoll (etwas breiter), very expressive
  (somewhat broader)
sehr breit, very broad
sehr gebunden, molto legato
sehr kurze Haltung, very short hold *(fermata)*
sehr langsam, gedehnt, very slow, expansive
sehr rasch (heftig), very quick (impetuous)
sehr stark, very strong, vigorous
sehr warm, in breiter Bewegung, very ardent,
  in a broad movement
sehr zart (und hell), very subdued (and distinct)
sehr zurücktretend, extremely restrained, held back
so leise als möglich, as soft as possible
so schwach als [also, *wie*] *möglich*, as delicate as possible
Sp(ieler), player
steigernd (beschleunigend), gradually louder (and faster)

Teilen, [divided into] parts (viz., "in 4 Teilen")

[die] übrigen get(eilt), the others divided *(gli altri, divisi)*
u(nd), and

verlangsamend (bis zum Schluss), slowing down (to the end)
viel rascher, beschleunigend, much quicker, accelerating
Viertel (etwas langsamer), quarter notes (somewhat slower)
von [vom], from, by, of
  [See "Other Tempo Markings" at the end of the glossary]

warm, warm, ardent
wechselt, changes, alternates
weich (u[nd] warm), delicate, tender (and warm)
weiter gedämpft, still muted
wenig, slightly
wieder, again, once more
wieder gedämpft, muted again
wieder gewöhnlich, return to the usual way of playing
  (modo ordinario)
wieder langsam(er), slow(er) once again
wieder lebhaft(er), lively (livelier) once again
wieder wie vorher, once again as before
wieder wie früher, once again as earlier

zaghaft, cautious, timid
zart, subdued, gentle
zögernd, hesitant
zu 2, both instruments (a²)
zurückhaltend, held back
zurücktreten, subsiding
zus(ammen), together *(unisono)*
zwei, two

Footnotes and Longer Score Notes

In *Pelleas und Melisande:*

Page 3, tempo:
  Die ♪ ein wenig bewegt—zögernd
  The ♪ a little agitated, but hesitant
Page 3, 1st bar, contrabassoon:
  Die in dieser Stimme vorkommenden Stellen der höchsten Tonlage sind, falls auf dem Ktr.-Fg. nicht ausführbar, durch Fagott zu ersetzen.
  If the passages in the highest register occurring in this part cannot be performed on the contrabassoon, substitute a bassoon.
Page 3, 1st bar, strings:
  in 2 gleichen Teilen pultweise
  in 2 equal parts, distributed by desk
Page 6, Fig. 3, horns:
  a 3 weich, aber bestimmt, hervortr.
  all three, softly but decidedly, to the fore
Page 34, Fig. 18 (and later), tempo:
  Wieder im Zeitmass
  Rasch anschwellend und beschleunigend
  A tempo
  Rapidly louder and faster
Page 38, footnote (for harp):
  Sollte dieser Gang nicht ausführbar sein, so lässt die 1. Harfe den Ton fis, die 2. Harfe den Ton a aus.

If this passage cannot be played, Harp 1 may omit the F-sharp, Harp 2, the A.
Page 50, after Fig. 30, tempo:
  1. Viertel zurückhaltend   2. u. 3. Viertel sehr rasch u. heftig.
  The 1st quarter note, held back; the 2nd and 3rd quarters, very quick and vigorous
Page 51, footnote (for trombones):
  Das "glissando" wird auf der Posaune folgendermassen ausgeführt: der Ton [♪] wird als Grundton (beziehungsweise Oktave) des 6. Zuges mit den Lippen fixiert und dann das Rohr durch alle Züge zusammengeschoben, doch so, dass die chromatischen, so wie die dazwischen-liegenden ¼ = ⅛ und kleinsten Intervalle deutlich hörbar sind, wie beim glissando der Streich-Instrumente.
  The glissando is performed on the trombone as follows: The note [♪] is fixed with the lips as the fundamental (or its octave) of the sixth position and then the slide is passed through all positions, but in such a way that the chromatic intervals as well as the quarter, eighth and smaller tones in between are clearly audible as in a string glissando.
Page 104, footnote (for clarinets):
  1. & 3. Klarinette womöglich wie geschrieben (Klang 4-gestrichenes C), falls nicht ausführbar, ist das Oktavzeichen wegzulassen

If possible, Clarinets 1 & 3 to play the notes as written (the actual sound: C above high C); if this cannot be done, the octave indication is to be ignored.

Page 105, Fig. 58, flutes:
die 3. grosse Flöte wechselt mit kleiner Flöte
Flute 3 alternates with Piccolo

Page 105, footnote (for clarinets):
1. & 3. Klarinette von hier an jedenfalls wie geschrieben.
Clarinets 1 and 3, from here on, definitely as written.

Page 110, last bar, flutes:
2. kleine Flöte wieder als 3. grosse Flöte
Piccolo 2 again changes to Flute 3

Page 124, footnote (for bass):
Kontrabass auf keinen Fall die höhere Octave spielen, event. auf D hinunterstimmen.
The bass must on no account play the higher octave; it may possibly be tuned down to D.

In *Five Orchestral Pieces:*

I: page 131, Fig. 4, cellos; after Fig. 5, violas:
*get. die 1. Hälfte arco [kurz, spiccato—mit Dämpfer]
die 2. Hälfte pizz.*
divisi, 1st half *arco* (short, *spiccato*) with mute
2nd half *pizz.*

I: page 131, footnote (for cellos):

Das 1. u. 2 Pult ⎫	*der Violoncelli immer der 1.*
Das 3. u. 4 Pult ⎭	*Spieler arco, der 2. Spieler pizz.*
Desks 1 and 2 ⎫	Cellos: At each desk, Player 1
Desks 3 and 4 ⎭	always plays *arco*, Player 2 plays *pizz.*

I: page 134, 1st bar, bass tuba:
mit Dämpfer, so stark wie möglich
muted, as strong as possible

I: page 134, footnote (for basses):
Das tiefe d muss dabei sein!
The low D must be present!

II: page 147, 3rd bar, solo viola:
äusserst zart, die Nebenstimmen entsprechend zarter
extremely delicate, the secondary voices correspondingly more delicate

II: page 153, 2nd bar, English horn:
wenn die Stelle nicht ppp möglich ist, bleibt sie weg; sie muss schwächer klingen als die Streicher
If the passage is not possible at *ppp*, it should be omitted; it must sound softer than the strings.

II: page 154, 2nd bar, basses:
4 Kontrabässe stimmen die G Saite auf Gis und spielen Flag.
4 basses tune the G string to G-sharp and play harmonics.

II: page 156, end, violas:
alle in 2 gleichen Teilen mit Dämpfer
Tutti, divisi a2, con sordino

III: page 157, footnote:
Es ist nicht Aufgabe des Dirigenten, einzelne ihm (thematisch) wichtig scheinende Stimmen in diesem Stück zum Hervortreten aufzufordern, oder scheinbar unausgeglichen klingende Mischungen abzutönen. Wo eine Stimme mehr hervorscheinen soll, als die anderen, ist sie entsprechend instrumentiert und die Klänge wollen nicht abgetönt werden. Dagegen ist es seine Aufgabe darüber zu wachen, dass jedes Instrument genau den Stärkegrad spielt, der vorgeschrieben ist; genau (subjektiv) seinem Instrument entsprechend und nicht (objektiv) sich dem Gesamtklang unterordnend.

*) *Der Wechsel der Akkorde hat so sacht zu geschehen, dass gar keine Betonung der einsetzenden Instrumente sich bemerkbar macht, so dass er lediglich durch die andere Farbe auffällt.*
It is not the conductor's task to call for individual voices in this piece that seem (theoretically) important to him to be played more prominently, or to tone down combinations that apparently sound unbalanced. Wherever a voice is to stand out above the rest, it is correspondingly scored and the sounds are not to be toned down. On the other hand, it *is* the conductor's task to take care that every performer plays at exactly the volume prescribed; exactly (subjectively) in accordance with his own instrument and not (objectively) subordinating himself to the total sound.

*) The change of chords must be executed so smoothly that absolutely no emphasis on the entering instruments can be felt, so that the change is merely perceptible through the difference in instrumental color.

III: page 158, Fig. 1, cellos:
4 Solo-Vcelli mit Dämpfer alle 4 auf der C-Saite
4 solo cellos with mute, all 4 on the C string

III: page 160, Fig. 4, footnote:
Jede Note genau so lang aushalten, wie vorgezeichnet; aber auch nicht länger!!!
Hold every note exactly as long as written, but not longer either!!!

III: page 161, 1st bar, basses:
1 fünfsaitiger Solo-Kb. auf der C-Saite
1 five-stringed solo bass on the C string

III: page 161, 2nd bar, cellos:
III. mit auf H herabgestimmter C-Saite
No. 3 with C string tuned down to B

IV: page 169, 1st bar, trombones:
Dieses A womöglich bringen, so stark es eben geht.
Play this A if possible, as loudly as can be done.

IV: page 171, 1st bar, cymbals:
tremolo auf einem Beckenteller mit einem Violoncellbogen
tremolo on one cymbal with a cello bow

Other Tempo Markings

nach und nach beschleunigend, steigernd, gradually quickening and growing louder
Nach und nach beschleunigend, gradually quickening
Etwas bewegter, somewhat more agitated
nach u(nd) nach ein wenig anschwellend, gradually growing a little louder
nach und nach etwas bewegter, gradually somewhat more agitated
nach und nach langsamer, gradually slower
nach und nach steigernd und anschwellend, gradually intensifying and growing louder
nach und nach wieder ins Tempo, gradually returning to original tempo

♩ = ♩ *vom Anfang*
♩ same as the beginning ♩

♩. = ♩ *vom früher*
♩. = the earlier ♩

♩. = ♩ *von vorher*
♩. = the previous ♩

Pelleas und Melisande

OP. 5 (1902–3)

Symphonic Poem for Orchestra
Based on Maurice Maeterlinck's Drama
Pelléas et Mélisande (1892)

Instrumentation

Piccolo [Kl. Fl. (*Kleine Flöte*)]
3 Flutes (Flute 3 doubles Piccolo 2) [gr. Fl. (*grosse Flöten*)]
3 Oboes (Oboe 3 doubles English Horn 2) [Ob. (*Oboen*)]
English Horn [E. H. (*Englischhorn*)]
E♭ Clarinet [Es-Klar. (*Es-Klarinette*)]
3 Clarinets in A, B♭ (Clarinet 3 doubles Bass Clarinet 2)
    [Klar. (A, B) (*Klarinetten*)]
Bass Clarinet in A, B♭ [Bss.-Klar. (A, B) (*Bass-Klarinette*)]
3 Bassoons [Fg. (*Fagotte*)]
Contrabassoon [Ktr.-Fg. (*Kontrafagott*)]

8 Horns in E, F [Hr. (*Hörner*)]
4 Trumpets in E, F [Trp. (*Trompeten*)]
Alto Trombone [Alt-Pos. (*Alt-Posaune*)]
4 Tenor-Bass Trombones [Ten.-Bss.-Pos. (*Tenor-Bass-Posaunen*)]
Contrabass Tuba [Ktrbss.-Ta. (*Kontra-Bass-Tuba*)]

4 Timpani [Pk., Pke., Pkn. (*"2 Paar Pauken"*)]
Percussion:
    Triangle [Trgl. (*Triangel*)]
    Cymbals, pair [Beck. (*"1 Paar Becken"*)]
    Tam-Tam [Tamt.]
    Large Tenor Drum [gr. Rhrtr. (*grosse Rührtrommel*)]
    Bass Drum [gr. Tr. (*grosse Trommel*)]
    Glockenspiel [Glocksp.]

2 Harps [Hrf., Hfe., Hrfn. (*Harfen*)]

16 1st Violins [I. Gge. (*Geigen*)]
16 2nd Violins [II. Gge. (*Geigen*)]
12 Violas [Br. (*Bratschen*)]
12 Cellos [Vcll. (*Violoncelli*)]
8 Basses [Ktrbss. (*Kontrabässe*)]

*) Die in dieser Stimme vorkommenden Stellen der höchsten Tonlage sind, falls auf dem Ktr.-Fg. nicht ausführbar, durch Fagott zu ersetzen

etwas zurückhaltend

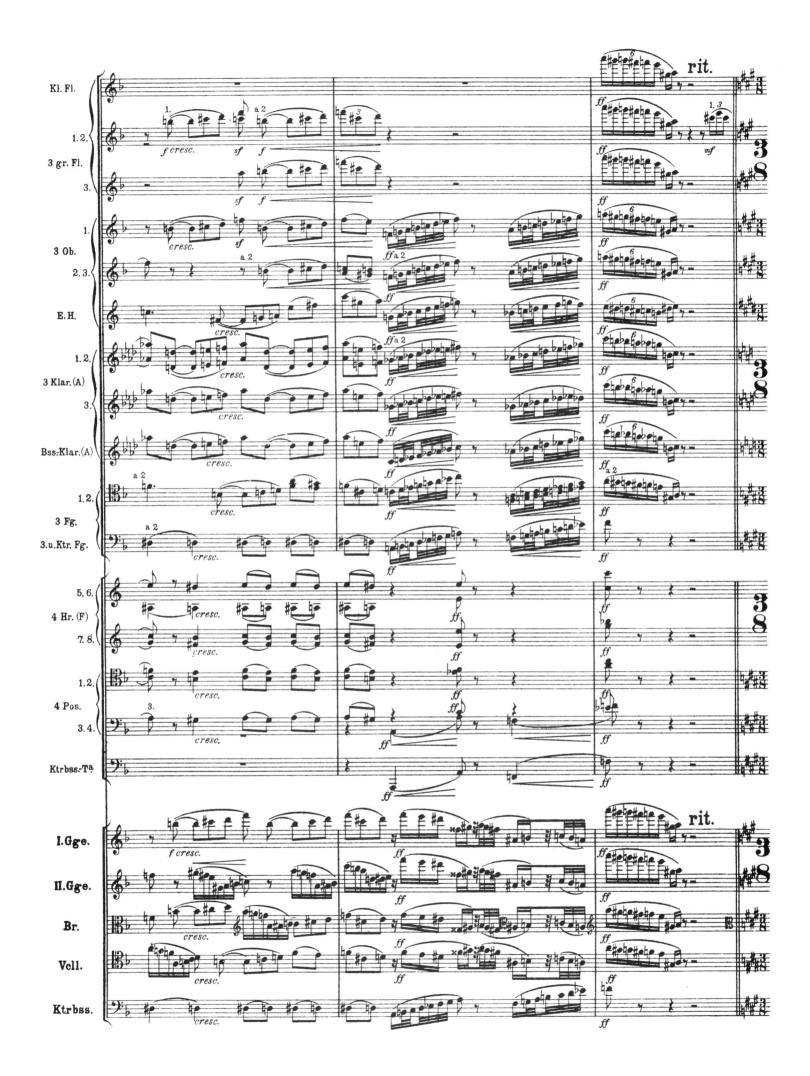

*) Sollte dieser Gang nicht ausführbar sein, so läßt die 1.Harfe den Ton *fis*, die 2.Harfe den Ton *a* aus.

Sehr langsam, gedehnt

Sehr langsam, gedehnt

*) Das „*glissando*" wird auf der Posaune folgendermaßen ausgeführt: der Ton 𝄢 wird als Grundton (beziehungsweise Oktave) des 6. Zuges mit den Lippen fixiert und dann das Rohr durch alle Züge zusammengeschoben, doch so, daß die chromatischen, sowie die dazwischen-liegenden 1/4 = 1/8 und kleinsten Intervalle deutlich hörbar sind, wie beim glissando der Streich-Instrumente

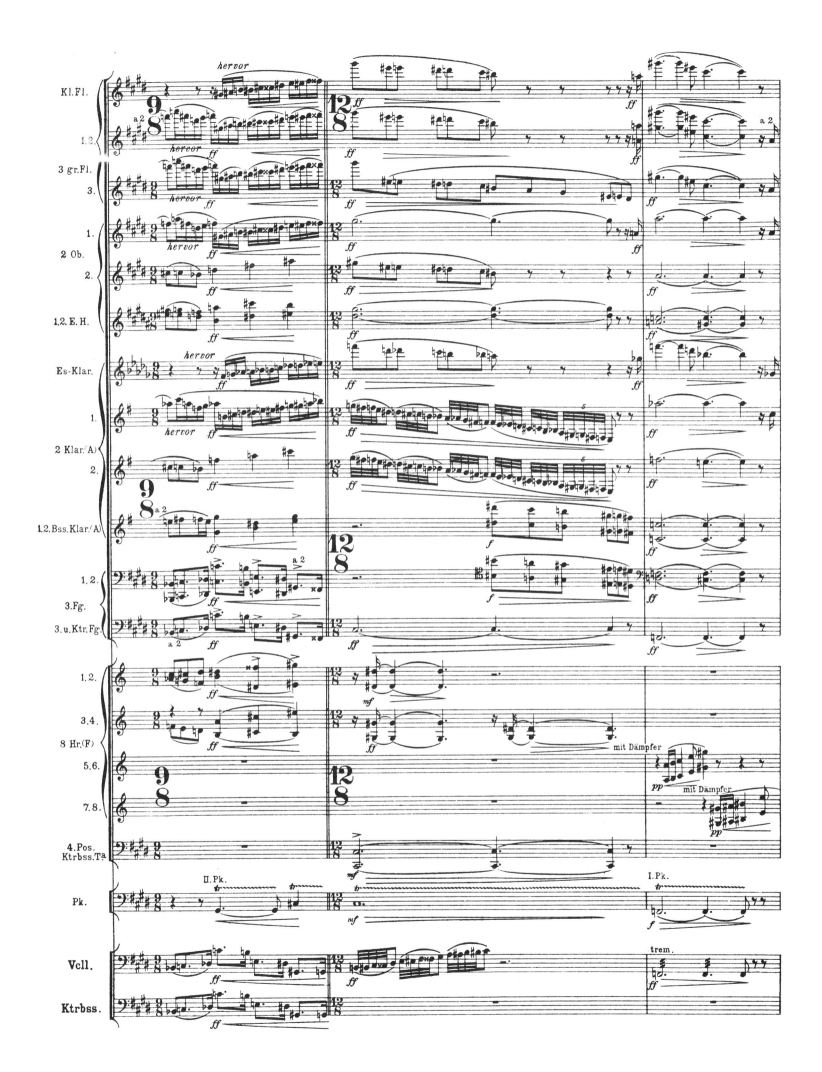

*)1.§ 3. Klarinette womöglich wie geschrieben (Klang 4-gestrichenes C) falls nicht ausführbar, ist das Oktavzeichen wegzulassen

nach und nach wieder ins Tempo

nach und nach wieder ins Tempo

*)Kontrabaß auf keinen Fall die höhere Octave spielen, event. auf D hinunterstimmen.

Five Orchestral Pieces
OP. 16 (1909)

Instrumentation

2 Piccolos [Kleine Flöten, Kl. Fl.]
3 Flutes [Grosse Flöten, Fl.]
3 Oboes [Oboen, Ob.]
English Horn [English Horn, Engl. H.]
4 Clarinets in D, A, B♭ [Klarinetten (D, A, B), Kl.]
Bass Clarinet in B♭ [Bassklarinette (B), Bkl.]
Contrabass Clarinet in A [Kontrabassklarinette (A), Kbkl.]
3 Bassoons [Fagotte, Fag.]
Contrabassoon [Kontrafagott, Kfag.]

6 Horns in F [Hörner (F), Hr.]
3 Trumpets in B♭ [Trompeten (B), Trp.]
4 Trombones [Posaunen, Pos.]
Bass Tuba [Basstuba, Btba.]

Percussion:
    Xylophone [Xylophon, Xyl.]
    Cymbals [Becken]
    Triangle [Triangel, Trgl.]
    Tam Tam [Tamtam, Tamt.]
    Timpani [Pauke, Pk.]
    Bass Drum [Gr(osse) Trommel, Gr. Trom.]

Harp [Harfe, Hrfe.]
Celesta [Celesta]

Violins I, II [Violinen, Viol.]
Violas [Viola]
Cellos [Violoncello, Vcello]
Basses [Kontrabass, Kb.]

I.

*) Das tiefe d muß dabei sein!

II. — Yester year

Schoenberg: op. 16, No. 3: Farben
Chord Scheme

Peabody Conservatory /JHU
Theory Classes [Mathews]

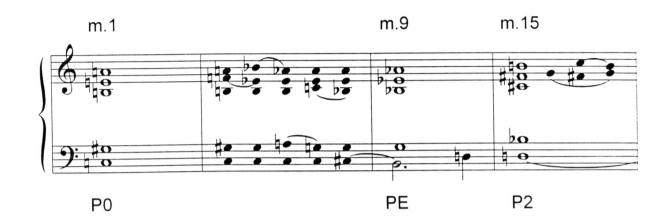

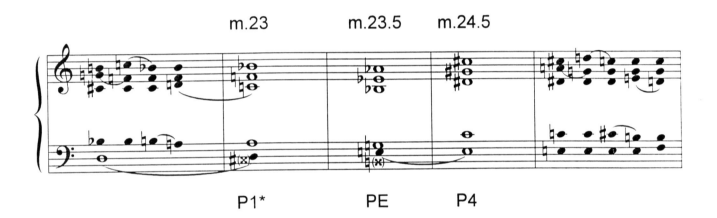

III. — Summer Morning by a Lake (colors)

Es ist nicht Aufgabe des Dirigenten, einzelne ihm (thematisch) wichtig scheinende Stimmen in diesem Stück zum Hervortreten aufzufordern, oder scheinbar unausgeglichen klingende Mischungen abzutönen. Wo eine Stimme mehr hervorscheinen soll, als die anderen, ist sie entsprechend instrumentiert und die Klänge wollen nicht abgetönt werden. Dagegen ist es seine Aufgabe darüber zu wachen, daß jedes Instrument genau den Stärkegrad spielt, der vorgeschrieben ist; genau (subjektiv) seinem Instrument entsprechend und nicht (objektiv) sich dem Gesamtklang unterordnend.

*) Der Wechsel der Akkorde hat so sacht zu geschehen, daß gar keine Betonung der einsetzenden Instrumente sich bemerkbar macht, so daß er lediglich durch die andere Farbe auffällt.

Jede Note genau so lang aushalten, wie vorgezeichnet; aber auch nicht länger!!!

IV.

Dieses A womöglich bringen, so stark es eben geht.

V. The obligatory Recitative

Hauptstimmen bezeichnet durch ⌈.

THE END